MANATEES

THE SEA MAMMAL DISCOVERY LIBRARY

Sarah Palmer

Rourke Enterprises, Inc.
Vero Beach, Florida 32964

Library of Congress Cataloging-in-Publication Data

Palmer, Sarah, 1955-
   Manatees.

   (The Sea mammal discovery library)
   Includes index.
   Summary: Describes, in simple terms, the
appearance, infancy, habits, behavior, and
habitat of the manatee or sea cow.
   1. Manatees—Juvenile literature. [1. Manatees]
I. Title.
II. Series: Palmer, Sarah, 1955-
Sea mammal discovery library.
QL737.S63P34   1989   599.5'5   88-26433
ISBN 0-86592-359-0

TABLE OF CONTENTS

MANATEES

Manatees are sometimes called "sea cows." They graze on plants in the water, just like a cow does on land. Like cows, manatees are very gentle and completely harmless. There are three **species** of manatees. One species lives in Africa, and the other two live in the Americas. The species most widely studied is the North American manatee (*Trichechus manatus*).

Manatees can wear their teeth down by grazing on sandy river beds

HOW THEY LOOK

Manatees are bulky, gray-brown, balloonlike creatures. Adult North American manatees can be 8 to 14 feet long and weigh up to two-thirds of a ton. Manatees have small heads surrounded by thick folds of skin. Their square snouts are dotted with stiff bristles. Manatees have no **hindlimbs**. Their **forelimbs** are well developed flippers that help them move easily through the water.

Manatees have well developed fore flippers

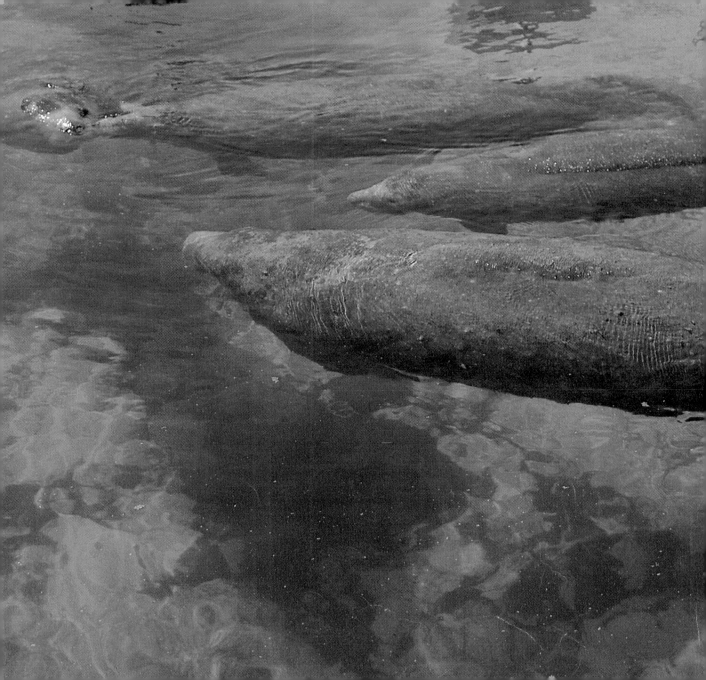

WHERE THEY LIVE

Manatees live only in warm, shallow waters. If the water becomes too cold in the **estuaries** they move inland to rivers and canals. Manatees can die if the water suddenly gets cold. North American manatees can be found in Florida, Central America, and the West Indian Islands. They live alone or in small groups. Manatees never venture onto land for any reason.

Manatees live in calm, sheltered waters

WHAT THEY EAT

Manatees are **vegetarians** and eat only plants. They are the only sea **mammals** that do not eat a lot of meat or fish. Manatees only eat fish if it is mixed in with the plants they are eating. They do not **prey** on other creatures. Manatees eat huge amounts of water plants like hydrilla, sea grasses, and water hyacinths. A 10 foot long manatee needs over 100 pounds of **vegetation** each day.

Manatees only eat plants

Manatees cruise along slowly, but they can hurry if they must

In muddy water it can be hard for manatees to see properly

HOW THEY EAT

Manatees' lips are split in two separate halves. Each half can move on its own. This makes it easy for manatees to grasp and eat water plants. Manatees chew a lot of grit and sand with their plants. That wears their teeth down, and they drop out. Luckily for the manatees, new teeth grow in to replace these worn out teeth. Scientists believe manatees may grow up to sixty new teeth in an average lifetime.

Manatees use their fore flippers to help guide food to their mouths

LIVING IN THE WATER

Manatees spend a lot of time swimming slowly through the water, feeding on plants. They spend nearly seven hours each day feeding. Manatees usually swim at a steady 2 to 6 M.P.H. They can move much more quickly if necessary. Scientists say their top speed is around 15 M.P.H. Manatees do not normally dive deeper than about 30 feet. They come to the surface to breathe about every four minutes.

Manatees need to breathe at the surface about every four minutes

THEIR SENSES

Manatees have good hearing and eyesight. Scientists think they may be farsighted. Manatees can see a long way ahead in clear water. However, sometimes they bump into objects close to them for no reason. In bayous and rivers, manatees' eyes can get scratched by sand and grit in the muddy water. A third eyelid closes over each eye to protect it. Manatees also have a well developed sense of touch. They often touch each other with their flippers.

Manatees often stay very close to one another

BABY MANATEES

Baby manatees are dark gray-brown at birth. Their skin lightens as they grow up. When they are born, manatees are about three feet long and weigh between 40 and 60 pounds. Manatee **calves** stay with their mothers for one or two years. The females teach their calves to breathe in water so they won't drown. Within three months the calves are grazing alongside their mothers.

Baby manatees stay with their mothers until they are two years old

MANATEES AND PEOPLE

People have always been a major threat to manatees. Many years ago people used to eat them. The manatees' thick skin was used to make leather, and their **blubber** was used for oil. Today manatees are protected by law, and people can no longer kill them. Even so, manatees are not always safe from people. Some people drive power boats over manatees because they do not see them. Many manatees are badly hurt, and some are even killed this way.

GLOSSARY

blubber (BLUH ber) — a thick layer of fat under the skin of a sea mammal

calves (KAV s) — baby manatees

estuaries (ES choo a rees) — places where rivers flow into the ocean

forelimbs (FORE LIMS) — front arms

hindlimbs (HIND LIMS) — back legs

mammals (MAM uls) — animals that give birth to live young and feed them with mother's milk

prey (PRAY) — to hunt other animals for food

species (SPEE seez) — a scientific term meaning type or kind

vegetarian (vej a TEAR ian) — an animal that only eats plants

vegetation (vej a TAY shun) — plant life

INDEX